Subsoil Plowing

**Two women, and the
beginning of
the Women's Rights Movement
in America**

poems by

Dorothy Brooks

Finishing Line Press
Georgetown, Kentucky

Subsoil Plowing

Two women, and the
beginning of
the Women's Rights Movement
in America

ACKNOWLEDGMENTS

The poem "Contemplating Marriage—1975" appeared in different form in
Alliance for the Arts Chapbook, Ft. Myers, FL, 2018.

The poems in this book are all based on actual historical events. The dates
given are approximate. Every attempt was made to be factually accurate, but
any errors of fact are mine and mine alone.   ~Dorothy Brooks

Publisher: Leah Maines
Editor: Christen Kincaid
Cover Art: Elizabeth Cady Stanton, seated, and Susan B. Anthony, standing,
three-quarter length portrait. [Between 1880 and 1902] Photograph.
Retrieved from the Library of Congress, <www.loc.gov/item/97500087/>.
Author Photo: Reg Brooks
Cover Design: Leah Huete

Printed in the USA on acid-free paper.
Order online: www.finishinglinepress.com
            also available on amazon.com

Author inquiries and mail orders:
Finishing Line Press
P. O. Box 1626
Georgetown, Kentucky 40324
U. S. A.

Table of Contents

This book is dedicated to
Susan B. Anthony (1820-1906)
and
Elizabeth Cady Stanton (1815-1902)
and all the other selfless women and men
who have fought to secure equal rights
for women

I LEARN WHAT IT MEANS TO BE A GIRL
Elizabeth Cady Stanton, 1827

I remember when my brother
died. My only brother.
His body laid out in the parlor.
I went to my father,
placed my head on his chest.
Look at me, I wanted to say,
I'm alive. I wanted
to make it up to him.
I knew I could do anything—
be anything—to please him.
I learned to ride, studied Greek,
Latin, won the top prize
at the Academy
ahead of all the boys.
I ran to him. At last,
he would see me,
see I was just as good
as any brother. He held me
at arm's length, gazed
into my eyes: "How I wish
you were a boy," he said.
The one thing I never could be.

THE NECKLACE
Elizabeth Cady Stanton, 1828

My twelfth Christmas,
my new coral necklace.
I wore it to show off,
and those boys, the future lawyers
my father taught, taunted me:

"Marry me, then the necklace
will be mine. I can sell it,
or give it away, even trade it
for a box of cigars!"

I appealed to my father.
"I'm afraid they are right.
It says so in these books."

"Then I'll burn those books!"

Father laughed. "Oh, my dear,
you'll have to learn to give speeches,
go up to Albany, convince
all those men to change the law."

It was beyond impossible,
they knew. It was a joke,
he and his students teasing me again.

*   *   *

And so it began. My father,
who never approved of my work,
set me on this path:
The Married Woman's Property Act
my first victory.

BOARDING SCHOOL DAYS
Susan B. Anthony, 1838

I want to learn
but not to leave behind
all I know:

Mother's quiet strength,
Father's wisdom,
my sisters, brother—
especially my sisters—

how I yearn for them,
for home,
for my old life.

These losses
will make me strong.

I must learn
independence.

A hard lesson.

HENRY STANTON
Elizabeth Cady Stanton, 1839

Autumn. Long rides
through the deepening countryside
with Henry Stanton:
A coolness to the air as the days grow short,
the slant of sunlight on turning leaves
casts the world in a golden glow.
His words to me as filled with sentiment
as the speeches he gives to crowded halls.
An abolitionist—my father
will never approve—
but Henry Stanton has my heart,
and though I insist we not *obey*,
we vow to love, to honor, to cherish,
from this day forward.

THE LADIES WERE NOT INVITED TO SPEAK

Elizabeth Cady Stanton, June, 1840
World Anti-Slavery Convention, London

but only to listen and learn,
as if we were unruly schoolchildren,
as if we didn't know every bit as much
about slavery as the men, as if
we had nothing to offer. They called
upon God himself, quoted Scripture,
it seemed the great celestial beings
were hovering with their blessing.
How could a convention charged
with securing the rights of slaves,
deny a voice to half of humanity?

And didn't I, on the long voyage over,
hold my own in every discussion,
every heated exchange? Henry
would say so. Our wedding journey,
and he loved the talk, the camaraderie,
loved having me by his side, joining in.

The convention's twelve days, exiled
to the balcony, were not all lost,
as I came to know Lucretia Mott,
a woman unafraid to speak aloud
all the feelings, opinions, and doubts
I held deep in my own heart. A woman
denounced in many of her own Quaker
communities for her radical vision.
We became fast friends.

THOUGHTS ON MARRIAGE
Susan B. Anthony, 1849

Twenty-nine years old,
my sisters, my friends, all gone,

disappeared
into marriage,

losing everything, even
their names.

I can't imagine myself
in that ill-fitting garment.

I am still discovering
who I am.

Found work as a teacher,
moved in with cousin Margaret,

but teaching is not for me,
and Margaret fell ill,

depended on me to care for her,
her baby as well, even her husband

full of Gold Rush dreams.
I soon became

their housemaid.
The unmarried woman:

*drudge and burden-
bearer of the family.*

If I were a man, I'd be off
to California.

CONTEMPLATING MARRIAGE—1975

His kitchen, late afternoon.
Sleeping appliances surround us.
The cooktop gleams.

I haven't said *yes* yet,
but I know I will.

Outside the window,
last leaves cling to their branches,
reds and yellows and oranges.

The sun sinks. Winter is coming,
but here it is warm. I imagine
I can see through the shadows

what lies ahead: years
of schoolbusses, lego-strewn carpet,
muddy socks, missed appointments,

but all I see in the darkening room
is his lovely face. Years from now
I will look back on this moment,

that pomegranate from the underworld
I plucked and ate, its sharp taste,
its singular pleasure.

SOJOURNER TRUTH

Susan B. Anthony, 1845

A woman. A slave.
Combining in herself
the two most despised
elements of humanity—
now standing tall,
speaking out.
How I wish I could have seen her.
And ain't I a woman?
Her voice clear and strong,
as the men in the hall snicker.
I've ploughed, planted,
gathered into barns.
Borne thirteen children,
seen most of 'em sold into slavery.
The crowd stilled,
listening to her words.
She dared them to laugh.
And ain't I a woman?
Now the men begin to applaud.
Even the ones who jeered
rise in tribute. A wise woman,
showing me the way.

WE MOVE TO SENECA FALLS, NEW YORK
Elizabeth Cady Stanton, 1848
"A healthy discontent is the first step to progress." ~ Emerson

Another baby. The household grows.
More cooking, washing, cleaning,
taking the children to doctors,
to school, finding teachers. How I long
for those days in Boston,
newly married, furnishing
the house, nursing my babies,
what fun it all was.
Gatherings of our friends,
reform work, these were pleasures
I loved and depended on.

Now here I am, miles
from town, muddy roads,
sick children. At last I understand,
this is the life most women live.
I find myself almost unable
to maintain the simplest order.

July, Lucretia Mott hosts a gathering
of women, earnest, thoughtful women.
A welcome reprieve!
I speak and speak, I find I can't
stop, all the discontent, yes, even
despair, of the last months pours out.
These women understand. These are lives
we all share. In this moment
the "Women's Rights Convention"
is born, born of simmering frustrations,
the will to change.

AFTER THE FIRST WOMEN'S RIGHTS CONVENTION
Seneca Falls, July 19-20, 1848
Elizabeth Cady Stanton

Ridicule. How can it be?
Our wonderful two days—
meetings, speeches, camaraderie,
every session crowded with women—
now mocked in the press.
We women dared
stand up and speak for ourselves.
Today we are denounced, shamed.
Voices rise against us
from the parlors to the pulpits.
Who can withstand such scorn:
Women back away. They concede.
Had I known this would happen,
would I have had the courage?

But now, something is begun.
It urges me forward
and I will not stop.
Finally able to speak my heart,
finally able to confess aloud
this festering discontent,
I am restored. Ready.

SUSAN B. ANTHONY MEETS ELIZABETH CADY STANTON, 1848

Susan B. Anthony, 1848

She speaks
so confidently.
Her face, her smile
invite me in.
She loves people,
it's plain to see.
Gracious, charming,
clearly someone
well versed
in the fine arts
of womanhood.
Our first meeting,
she's rushing off
to engagements:
houseguests,
children,
dinner, bedtime.
And yet, her eyes
betray an uncommon
intelligence, a spirit
that will not quit.

Elizabeth Cady Stanton,* 1848

There she stood.
With her good, earnest face,
genial smile,
dressed in gray with pale blue ribbons,
the perfection of neatness and sobriety.
Susan B. Anthony.
I liked her thoroughly.

*A "found poem" adapted from Elizabeth Cady Stanton's
autobiography, *Eighty Years and More*

PROTECTION
Susan B. Anthony, 1858

They say I need
protection,

a woman alone
is not safe.

They say I need a man
for—what?

Protection from what?
Other men? Predators?

I have travelled this state,
this country

alone,

with other women,
sometimes men,

unharmed.
Women are fearful.

They've been told
a husband will keep them

safe.

They never learn
their own strength.

They never learn
no one is safe.

MRS. PHELPS
Susan B. Anthony, 1860

She came to me
veiled,
as hunted as a runaway
slave—
a runaway wife.
Spoke of her husband
the Senator,
his multiple affairs,
his abuse—
he confined her
to the asylum—
her eventual escape.
Here she was
with her daughter
needing protection,
defying the law:
she had no legal right
to her own child.
But those men,
those righteous
abolitionists,
who would break any law for a slave,
refused:
Marriage. Divorce. Custody.
Too radical.
Easy to condemn
a distant plantation owner.
Impossible to stand against
one of their own.
Only my father understood.
Only my father
agreed,
but like me
could do nothing.
Mrs. Phelps, I am so sorry.

THE DINNER PARTY
Elizabeth Cady Stanton, 1860

I was raised a proper young lady.
I know my place. I know
to let the men prevail. But I can never
keep quiet, especially when the talk
turns to Women's Rights. Last night
I held forth as if leading a convention,
my arguments solid, my logic firm.
The ladies at the table were silent.
I saw their faces, stoic, as the men joked,
disagreed, defended, but I carried on.
After dinner, invited to join the ladies,
I would sooner have slipped out the side door,
so great was my embarrassment.
Once in the parlor, they approached,
one after another, thanked me
for my words, and for my work—
In spite of their silence.
                              Sometimes
I don't know where I belong.

CENSURED—2017

"She was warned. She was given an explanation.
Nevertheless, she persisted."
Mitch McConnell rebuking Elizabeth Warren
on the floor of the United States Senate

Ninety-one degrees outside
and that old woman
on the metro train
is dressed in a full burka.
Mousy brown cloth
covers her head, her mouth,
her whole body.
Only her eyes are visible.

Last month I watched
a woman, a senator,
speak out
on the floor of the Senate
after those men,
her fellow senators,
voted to shut her up.
She was strong, confident.
Refused to be silenced.
I was proud to be a woman.

I want to say to that old woman,
Someone taught you that,
taught you female bodies
are shameful, must be
concealed, they induce men
to sin—sin?

                    Is sin a word
she would use?
Or is it my own.
I, too, was taught
men can't control themselves
in the presence of a woman
wearing the wrong clothes.

That poor woman,
faceless, voiceless.
I'm sure she believes
her God blesses her
for hiding her body,
hiding her self.
I expect she is a good woman,
following all the rules.

Perhaps she knows
the price women pay,
even today,
for speaking out.

MOTHER
Susan B. Anthony, 1857

Blind.
Like everyone else
I didn't see you
there, taking care.
Always there.
Your life—
your invisible, necessary life.
The only life you could choose.

THE NEW, TRUE WOMAN
Susan B. Anthony, 1857*

Will not be exponent of another
Or allow another to be such for her
Will be her own individual self
Will stand or fall on her own
Individual wisdom and strength

Reverently laid aside will be the old ideas—
Man was made for himself woman for him
Man is the oak she the vine
He is the head she the heart
He the great conservator of wisdom
She of love—

Woman equally with man
Made for her own individual happiness
Made to develop every power of her nature
To use every talent given her by God
In the great work of life
To the best advantage of herself and the race.

*A "found" poem adapted from her speech, "True Womanhood"

RIFT, BETRAYAL, DEFEAT
PASSAGE OF THE 14TH AMENDMENT—1868
Susan B. Anthony and Elizabeth Cady Stanton, a conversation

We are abandoned!

> The 14th Amendment will pass without us.
> For the first time "male" is enshrined
> in the Constitution. Negro *men* will vote.
> Women, Negro or white, will not.

Our movement is fractured.
Wendell Phillips proclaims
This the Negro's hour!
Women, he says, have power
through their men.
What need have they
of the vote?

> And who was it stood by the slave?
> Who was it fought side by side,
> spoke out, led meetings, signed petitions?
> Abolition was our cause. Freedom.
> Equal rights for all: *female* slaves
> as well as male, *women* as well as men.

Throughout the war
we were silent.
Four long years.
We sacrificed,
supported the cause,
certain a victory
would bring suffrage
to all. Now they say
the Negro man
deserves equality.
Deserves the vote.
Later for women.

> Fredrick Douglass, our champion,
> tells us to wait our turn. Be patient,
> he says, your day will come.

Patience?
We've been
patient. I'm sick
of being told to wait.

The door is open now.
If it closes, who can say
when it will open again.

We, too, are citizens.
All we ask
is respect, dignity—
the vote.

Only the vote can assure freedom.
Only the vote can secure rights.
Only the vote can guarantee equality.

Though you and I
stand alone,
I will never support
suffrage
for some
and not for all.

Though you and I stand alone,
I will not stop, I will not rest
until women have the vote.

REFLECTIONS: 50 YEARS OF FRIENDSHIP

MY FRIEND, SUSAN B. ANTHONY
Elizabeth Cady Stanton, 1898

They say we are so different
and they are right—Susan
is my better self. She's my good angel
always goading me to work,
the thorn in my side.

Without her constant prodding
I may have become a woman content
to spend my days absorbed,
as most women are,
in the care of home and children.
She reminds me of who I am.

Different? Perhaps.
But my passion for the cause
rivals hers. In this, there is
no difference between us.
None at all.

MY FRIEND, MRS. STANTON
Susan B. Anthony, 1898

She listens to my ideas
shapes them
into fine language,
speaks these words
to great halls
in the way I wish
I was able.
Those hours
at her kitchen table
devising plans,
editing speeches,
holding one of her babies,
laughing together
at the "sons of Adam,"
are among
my happiest memories.
I am the reformer
I've become
because she
was by my side.

SUBSOIL PLOWING
Susan B. Anthony

I have all the rights I need,
the woman said
as she refused my petition,
slammed the door.

I understand.
Once I, too, believed it:
women spoke
in our Quaker meeting
without censure.
Father encouraged me
and all my sisters
in our education.
I was a teacher,
with my own salary.
I had all the rights
I needed.

My mother could have
told me. Instead,
she went along.
Silently.

How far I have come
since leaving home.

Mrs. Stanton helped me
understand:
to see the limits
and the burdens
of the law.

She will never be one of those
quietly accepting.
I do love her for that.

These beliefs run deep.
The work I do
is subsoil plowing.
It may not bear fruit
in my lifetime.

2016—DEAR SUSAN, I VOTED TODAY

the same way I've voted every year.
It was nothing special. No one stopped me,
or yelled obscenities. I didn't end up
like you, handcuffed, or in jail.
It's been almost one hundred years now,
that women were treated like ordinary citizens,
allowed to vote alongside the men.
Voting is not something I've had to fight for.

But today was different. Today,
as I climbed the steps to the courthouse,
walked the marble hallway, stood in line,
marked my ballot, I thought of you,
your courage, your tenacity.
I thought of the years
you spent lecturing, petitioning,
traveling this whole country,
not for yourself alone, but for us,
the women that would come after you,

for me. Because today I voted
for a woman
to be president of these United States.
The highest office in the land.
Other countries, Germany, England,
have women leaders. Maybe it's our time.
Almost a century. It's finally time.

FAILURE IS IMPOSSIBLE * —2017

Just think of it: I have been striving for over sixty years
for a little bit of justice no bigger than that,
yet I must die without obtaining it.
　　　　　　Susan B. Anthony, on her deathbed, 1906

In the dream, she's having coffee with me
looking just the way she does on TV:
lime green pantsuit, make-up, hair in place,
as if she's ready for another day
on the campaign trail. Quiet. Thoughtful.
She looks tired. People wander about
the coffee shop. No one notices,
as if we are invisible. *It's hard*
to get out of bed in the morning,
she says, not looking up. *The children,*
she smiles, *my two grandchildren,*
they are the only reason. So many times
she's had to get up and start again.
We both know there won't be another.
I'd like to ask what she thinks
of the country now. Instead
I honor her silence, sit with her,
until the light comes in the window,
and it's not a coffee shop at all
but my familiar bedroom. The image
is still so clear, so real, like a memory.
It lingers. I don't want to leave it behind.
A quiet feeling, like hers. Resigned.
Another generation will have to carry on.

* "Failure is Impossible" are the last words Susan B. Anthony spoke in
public, at her 86th birthday celebration, 1906.

IN THE WOMEN'S ROOM—2017

The young girl beside me
smiles at the mirror
as she combs her long, dark hair
after the boat races.

I won, she says to me,
our faces reflected side by side,
a generation or more
between us. *I love sailing,
riding the waves, the feel
of the wind. I love,*

she turns to me now
like this is a secret we share,
to beat the boys! Only fifteen.
I see her excitement, her passion,

and my heart aches
remembering—
the difficulties, the cost.
So many hard choices.

She gathers her hair
into a ponytail, tosses her head
as our eyes meet again:

It is a secret we share,
a bond I'm proud to share.

Dorothy Howe Brooks' work has appeared or is forthcoming in numerous literary magazines, most recently in *Tampa Review, Atlanta Review, Poet Lore, Louisiana Literature, Broad River Review,* and *Chariton Review.* Her second chapbook, *Interstices,* was published in 2009 by Finishing Line Press, and her full length poetry collection, *A Fine Dusting of Brightness,* was published in 2013 by Aldrich Press. She teaches "Writing Poetry" in the LifeLong Learning Institute at Florida Southwestern State College in Punta Gorda, Florida.